Write It Right

Writing a
Blog

By Cecilia Minden

Published in the United States of America by
Cherry Lake Publishing
Ann Arbor, Michigan
www.cherrylakepublishing.com

Reading Adviser: Marla Conn MS, Ed., Literacy specialist, Read-Ability, Inc.
Book Designer: Felicia Macheske
Character Illustrator: Carol Herring

Photo Credits: © szefei/Shutterstock, 5; © Zurijeta/Shutterstock, 7; © Brocreative/Shutterstock.com, 17

Graphics Throughout: © simple surface/Shutterstock.com; © Mix3r/Shutterstock.com; © Artefficient/Shutterstock.com; © lemony/Shutterstock.com; © Svetolk/Shutterstock.com; © EV-DA/Shutterstock.com; © briddy/Shutterstock.com; © IreneArt/Shutterstock.com

Library of Congress Cataloging-in-Publication Data has been filed and is available at catalog.loc.gov

Cherry Lake Publishing would like to acknowledge the work of The Partnership for 21st Century Skills.
Please visit www.p21.org for more information.

Printed in the United States of America
Corporate Graphics

Table of
CONTENTS

CHAPTER ONE

What Is a Blog?

Keeping a **blog** is like writing in a journal. In a journal, your writing is private. You might even keep it locked away. But on the Web, other people can see your writing.

Blogs let people know what you are doing or thinking. What interesting things are happening on your sports teams? In class? At your after-school club? All of these can be discussed on a blog!

Perhaps your class is planting a vegetable garden.

Writing a blog can be fun!

Brainstorm Ideas

In this activity, you will make a list of possible subjects for your blog.

INSTRUCTIONS:

1. Think about the things you do in your classroom or community.
2. Think about what would be fun to write about.
3. Ask your friends for their thoughts.
4. Choose a topic!

Sample List

- My principal got a new puppy.
- My school's spelling team won a national competition.
- My class planted a vegetable garden. ✓

A blog about your favorite books can help
others choose books for themselves.

CHAPTER TWO

Parts of a Blog

Blogs can have several designs and **layouts**. But all blogs share some of the same features.

The **URL** is the address to your website. It is what a person types in to visit your blog. Open up a web browser. You can find the URL at the top of your screen.

The header and blog title will show up at the top of each page of your blog. Some websites also let you give your blog a subtitle. A subtitle gives more information.

Most of your screen will show the **body** of the blog. This is the area where blog **posts** are shown. Posts are made up of **text** or images. Each post gets its own title. It also has the date the blog post was written. Underneath the blog post, readers can write **comments**.

Some blogs have sidebars. These are tall, thin panels on the side of the screen. You might find links to other websites or older blog posts there.

Look How Our Garden Grows
A Class Blog

BLOG TITLE

BLOG SUBTITLE

POSTED ON Date • AUTHORED BY Noah

DATE AND AUTHOR

POST TITLE

POST TITLE

Your blog post goes here. You can type as much or as little as you like.

SIDEBARS ARE HERE

POST

COMMENTS
Readers can comment on your blog here.

COMMENTS

SIDEBARS

CHAPTER THREE

Name Your Blog

You can ask your parents to help you set up a blog using a site like www.blogger.com or www.wordpress.com. At school, your teacher might use a website such as www.kidblog.org.

ACTIVITY

Make It Official

In this activity, you will pick a title for your blog and then create a URL.

INSTRUCTIONS:

1. Choose a title for your blog. Pick a title that tells people something about you or your topic.

2. Once you have a title, you can pick a URL for your blog.

   - Pick your URL carefully. Every blog must have a different URL. You should brainstorm backup choices in case someone is already using the URL you want.

A GARDEN BLOG

- Room 19 Grows Vegetables!
- Growing Our Dinner!
- Very Good Veggies
- Look How Our Garden Grows ✓

Sample URL list

- http://room19garden.blogspot.com
- http://gradeschoolgarden.wordpress.com ✓
- http://verygoodvegetables.blogspot.com

CHAPTER FOUR

Make It POP!

Once your blog has been created and named, it's time to pick out a design. Every blogging site offers many **templates** or **themes** to choose from. They help to create the look of your blog. Find one with colors, a layout, and pictures that match what you are writing about.

You want your blog to catch the attention of your reader. Use colors that will be noticed. Keep your blog clean and free of clutter.

Crafting a Design

In this activity, you will come up with a design for your blog.

INSTRUCTIONS:

1. Consider your topic, title, and URL.
2. Make a list of colors that go with your theme.
3. Make a list of images that might be helpful to display.

Sample Design Ideas

COLORS

- Greens ✓
- Browns
- Oranges

PICTURES

- Students measuring out the garden plot
- Students looking over packets of seeds
- Students working a garden that is showing some green shoots ✓

CHAPTER FIVE

Writing Your First Blog Post

Your blog is set up and ready to go. Are you ready to write?

Every blog post has two parts: a title and a body. The title is a lot like a newspaper headline. It should say what your post is about. The body is the main part of the post. It contains your words, photos, videos, and more.

In your first blog post, say hello and explain why you are starting a blog.

Talk with an adult about what should and shouldn't be posted on a blog. You should not post personal information such as last names, addresses, or phone numbers.

ACTIVITY

Writing Your First Blog

In this activity, you will write your first post. This post will inform readers about your blog. It will also tell them what to expect in future postings.

INSTRUCTIONS:

1. Write the title of the blog post. You want to get your readers' attention, so keep it short and lively.
2. Start with a short introduction. You want to let your readers know what they will be learning about.
3. Now work on the body of your post. This will be where you explain everything that has happened so far.
4. End with a conclusion. Let your readers know what they can expect in the next post.

Look How Our Garden Grows
A Class Blog

POSTED ON: April 23, 2019, by Noah

TITLE: **Room 19 Really Digs Gardening!**

INTRODUCTION:

Welcome to Room 19. A few weeks ago, Mrs. B told us we were going to plant a vegetable garden! She told us we will plan out and design the garden, plant the seeds, and tend the garden. We will use our skills in reading, math, and science to do all of this. We can even use art skills to decorate a scarecrow to keep the birds away!

BODY:

Our first step was planning out the garden. We took a class vote to grow four vegetables: carrots, tomatoes, lettuce, and corn. No one wanted to grow peas!

Our parents helped us turn over the soil. That was great because digging is really hard work. At last our garden was ready for us to start planting.

We are now working on marking off the garden plot with stakes and string.

CONCLUSION:

Come back to this blog next week to see how we set up the garden. Happy growing!

CHAPTER SIX

Blog Comments

Blogs are fun to write. They are also fun to read! Did you read a blog post that you really liked? You can tell the author how much you enjoyed it. Most blogs let readers write comments at the bottom of the posts. This can turn a blog into a conversation between an author and a reader.

When you write a comment, be polite. Choose words that won't hurt the author's feelings. Try to be helpful.

It is fun to share interesting blogs with friends.

Sometimes an author will ask readers for their thoughts about the blog. The author might ask for suggestions on how to improve it. Your comments should give helpful suggestions.

Constructing Comments

In this activity, you will create a list of helpful and not helpful comments.

INSTRUCTIONS:

1. Make two columns on a sheet of paper.
2. At the top of the left column, write "Comments that help."
3. At the top of the right column, write "Comments that need work."
4. Place the sample comments below where you think they fit best. Which comments would you want on your blog?

- The video of students working in the garden is inspiring! Please post more videos.

- I don't like to eat vegetables.

- Good job on demonstrating how to lay out a garden!

- The close-up photo looks great!

- This is boring.

COMMENTS THAT HELP

- The video of students working in the garden is inspiring! Please post more videos.

- The close-up photo looks great!

- Good job on demonstrating how to lay out a garden!

COMMENTS THAT NEED WORK

- I don't like to eat vegetables.

- This is boring.

CHAPTER SEVEN

Updating Your Blog

Now you know how to set up, write, and read blogs. The last step is to keep writing! You need to schedule a regular time to update your blog. You want to include current information, videos, pictures, and interviews.

Most importantly, have fun!

GLOSSARY

blog (BLAWG) a web page that is like an online journal, where you can easily add new information

body (BAH-dee) the main area of a blog post, where you include text, audio, photos, or videos

comments (KAH-ments) readers' written responses to a blog post

layouts (LAY-outs) ways of organizing information, images, and other elements on a web page

posts (POHSTS) entries in a blog

templates (TEM-pluhts) premade layouts for a blog that includes colors, images, and designs

text (TEKST) words

themes (THEEMZ) designs for a web page

URL (YOO AR EL) stands for Uniform Resource Locator, another way of saying web address

INFORMATION

BOOKS

Cornwall, Phyllis. *Mind Your Manners Online*. Ann Arbor, MI: Cherry Lake, 2012.

Mack, James. *Journals and Blogging*. Chicago, IL: Raintree, 2009.

Raatma, Lucia. *Blogs*. Ann Arbor, MI: Cherry Lake, 2010.

WEBSITES

Kidblog
http://kidblog.org
This site allows teachers to set up free, safe blogs for kids in their classroom.

Mrs. Yollis' Classroom Blog
http://yollisclassblog.blogspot.com
Visit Mrs. Yollis's third-grade class online. This blog won the Edublog Award for Best Class Blog in 2011. You can see the class blog and links to students' individual blogs.

INDEX

About the AUTHOR

Cecilia Minden, PhD, is the former director of the Language and Literacy Program at Harvard Graduate School of Education. She earned her doctorate from the University of Virginia. While at Harvard, Dr. Minden also taught several writing courses. Her research focused on early literacy skills and developing phonics curriculums. She is now a literacy consultant and the author of over 100 books for children. Dr. Minden lives with her family in McKinney, Texas. She would like to thank the Burdette kids for giving her ideas for her books.